Written by Beverly Harris

Copyright 2018 By Beverly Harris

All rights reserved. No part of this book may be reproduced or transmitted in any form or by any means, electronic or mechanical including photocopying, recording, or by any information storage and retrieval system, without written permission from the copyright owner.

This is a fiction work. Names, characters, places and incidents either are the product of the authors imagination or used fictitiously, and any resemblance to any actual persons living or dead, events, or locales is entirely coincidental.

Cover art created by Natasha Hamuene

ISBN: 978-1-7325911-5-8

Jamestown Tobacco Boy
Dream of Freedom

Jamestown Tobacco Boy Dream of Freedom

This is the story of a boy who found a way to use the mystical powers of his mind and his courage to escape his realm and live his dream. The seed of this feat had been planted early in his life and it was watered often so that it sprouted roots and flourished until we find it on a hot June day in 1679 near maturity in the boy, named Daniel who was hard at work chopping weeds in one of the many tobacco fields that grew on the plantation that he lived on outside of Colonial Jamestown, Virginia.

Daniel, who had turned twelve the month before was a slave of African descent. He was rather tall for his age and like most who don't get enough to eat, he was very slim. He had deep brown colored skin and thick dark hair. Also, like most boys his age Daniel was full of hopes and dreams. Daniel's dream was to have his freedom. He thought day in and day out about what it would be like to be free and to have the opportunity to make a good life for himself and his mother, who was also a slave.

A man that Daniel called Master Rob owned him, his mother, and the other slaves who lived on the plantation with him. Master Rob was a tall, wiry man with dark hair and a fiery disposition. He had been born in England some thirty-odd years ago and had accompanied his parents Will and Elizabeth to the colonies in 1659, after his father received a bequeath of 100,000 acres of land from the king. Master Rob took over the running of the plantation after his father, died in 1670. He and his father, like most of the other plantation owners, had amassed a fortune on the sale of tobacco that was produced using the free labor of Daniel and the other slaves.

Although the slaves worked hard doing the backbreaking labor, they did not share in any of the comforts that their efforts brought to the plantations. They suffered a meager, existence in which they lacked the very basics of life; like enough food to fill their stomachs or a decent roof over their heads.

There were no laws to force Master Rob or the other slave owners to pay them, or to protect them from harsh treatment. So, they were forced to work long hours doing the will and work of their owners without being paid a cent.

Slaves like Daniel's mother Becca, who was a seamstress. She could have earned a handsome salary, and she and Daniel could have lived quite well if she had been allowed to keep any of her wages. But because she was a slave, she was neither paid by Master Rob for any of the work that she did for his family, nor was she allowed to keep anything that she earned for the work that she did when she was rented out to work for others.

She was never even allowed the time or any of the left-over fabric scraps to make decent clothes for herself or for Daniel. She was forced to watch her son wear ragged, threadbare clothing while she worked day after day creating beautiful garments for others.

Becca was a small, mocha complexioned woman, of few words. Her rough gnarled fingers resembled miniature dried sticks and told the tale of a lifetime of hard work of sewing and field and house work. Extremely talented, she spent countless hours making elaborate dresses, gowns, skirts, shirts, and bonnets for Master Rob's wife, Mistress Cissy, and for their children, Ned and Clarisse.

The mistress, who had come from a wealthy English family, was accustomed to wearing the latest and finest fashions. She ordered bolts of the most expensive silk, velvet, brocade, and broadcloth fabrics from England and France and had Becca sew them into elaborate finery for herself and for her children.

Becca often embroidered detailed patterns onto the sleeves, hems, and bodices of the dresses and gowns that she made for the mistress. She trimmed the collars and sleeves of the shirts and dresses with lace that she created from fine threads. The mistress was especially particular about her bonnets. She insisted that all of them be made of velvet and trimmed with flowers that Becca constructed of silk ribbons and attached to the bonnets with delicate stitches.

Daniel loved his mother, but he never had the chance to spend much time with her. They both worked from sun up to sun down. His mother was often required to stay overnight at Master Rob's house to cook and help serve food when he and Mistress Cissy entertained.

There was one time a while back that Daniel had been allowed to accompany her to work. It was when the master was giving a big party on a cold night. It had been Daniel's job that night to chop wood and to keep the fires going in all of the fireplaces in the dining room and in the parlors. That night Daniel chopped the wood and had it neatly stacked on the back porch. He was reaching to pick some up to carry into the kitchen because Becca had told him that more wood was needed for the wood-burning stove, when Seth who was one of the slaves that worked in the house, asked him to see to the fireplace in the big parlor at the front of the house. "Mind your manners, keep quiet and be quick," Seth told him.

Daniel picked up his full wood bucket and moved quickly and carefully down the long hallway that connected the main rooms of the first floor of the house and entered the parlor. The fireplace was at the far end of the room. Daniel saw that the fire was nearly out. He walked over and threw several fresh logs on top of the smoldering charred logs that were in the fireplace and then picked up the fire poker from its stand and used it to prod and move the logs around. Sparks flew in the air, the fire re-ignited, and expanded into brilliant flames.

Daniel put the poker back and looked up over the fireplace for the first time to see a large portrait of a white-haired man dressed in a beautiful, red velvet cloak with a fur collar around his neck. On his head, the man in the portrait wore a gold crown. Daniel had never seen anyone dressed in such finery, and stared at the picture for a moment before he remembered that he needed to get back to work. He picked up the now empty bucket and headed back to the kitchen where he met Seth who asked him, "Did you get that fire tended?" "Yes sir," Daniel told him. "Good Daniel, you didn't leave no mess in that room, did you?" "No sir, I didn't leave a mess. I emptied the wood, and I came back just like you told me to do. I only stood a minute looking at the picture of the man over the fireplace. Who is that man in the picture, Seth?" "I don't know for sure, but I heard the mistress tell one of her lady friends one time that he was some kind of king or something from a far off land that I never heard tell of before. Now, you best stop asking questions and get back to your work before someone gets the idea that we loafing." He smiled, winked at Daniel, and walked hastily away to attend to the candles in another part of the house.

Daniel had not seen his master on that night, nor did he see much of Master Rob on most days. To Daniel, it seemed like the man must have spent most of his time sitting on top of Jacque, his big chestnut brown horse, because that was where he was every time that Daniel saw him. Master Rob rarely spoke to the slaves directly. He would tell the slave overseer Mr. Joe what he wanted the slaves to get done. Mister Joe who had come to the colony from England about ten years before, was a short stout man who, being obsessed with the idea of becoming a plantation owner someday, reveled in the authority of his overseer position. Master Rob paid him to stay out in the fields with the slaves while they worked. And he was the one who made sure that the slaves did all of the work that Master Rob assigned, and that the work was completed to his employers' satisfaction.

On that June day, in the middle of a steamy afternoon; the sun overhead had created a haze that you could see if you looked up. But Daniel did not look up at the sun. He knew better than to be seen doing anything other than his work. The slaves had been working in that field since early morning. Jip, Mister Joe's large brown and white hunting dog, lay dozing in the hot sun near Sabra, the oldest slave on the plantation. Sabra was sitting in the dirt at the end of one of the rows of tobacco plants. Daniel and the other slaves could hear the *tat, tat, tat* sound from Sabra's drum as he softly patted it, creating a steady rhythm.

He was made to play the drums because Mister Joe believed that the drumbeat somehow made the other slaves work faster. Sabra was a smart man. He was viewed by most as powerless, but he used this misconception and the fact that he was forced to play the drums in a powerful way. He used the drums to help Daniel and the other slaves by sending discreetly coded messages in his beats and songs.

Sabra was old and he moved slowly. He walked with a stoop that came from many years of bending to work in the fields. He limped slightly because he had fallen from a wagon and broken his leg a few years ago. The broken leg had gone largely untreated, which left him with an odd gait that made walking very difficult. His job was to do chores, take messages for Master Rob, and to play the drums. Both Master Rob and Mister Joe thought that Sabra was pretty close to worthless because he was too slow to help with the tobacco. Since he could still do a few things, they kept him on the plantation. They thought he would die soon, and figured that they would get whatever work out of him that they could for as long as he lived.

Sabra who was born in Angola, was a young man when he and twenty or so other Africans arrived in August of 1619 aboard a ship called "The White Lion" at a port that was known then as Point Comfort. It is now located on Fort Monroe, in Hampton Virginia. The ship out of provisions, had docked at Point Comfort to restock; trading its captives for food and supplies. Sabra and the others were taken off of the ship and forced into indentured servitude.

Sabra at some point had somehow ended up as a slave on the plantation. But he never told Daniel much about that time on the ship or how he had ended up on the plantation and Daniel never asked about it. Daniel thought that those must have been difficult times for Sabra and that Sabra would have told him about them if he had wanted him to know.

But Sabra did tell Daniel about what it was like to grow up in Africa; and he taught Daniel games, like kick ball that he had played when he was a boy. The time that Daniel spent with Sabra was his happiest. Sabra was like a wise and jovial grandfather to Daniel. Sabra told Daniel about his boyhood in Africa because he wanted Daniel to understand that there was a world outside of the plantation and outside of the colonies; a world in which people were not forced to be slaves because of the color of their skin. He wanted Daniel to understand that his situation of enslavement was absurd, and that places existed where people of all colors enjoyed freedom.

Sabra told Daniel, "When I was a boy, I ran and played with my friends in the lands around my village. The land was very rich and beautiful. The tree limbs there drooped with the heaviness of all kinds of sweet, ripe fruits. When my friends and I played and became hungry, we would stop to pick it and eat until we were full. Or sometimes we played on the beach where the water was so clear that it shimmered like blue and green jewels when the sun shone on it. We would catch huge fish and take them to our homes where our mothers would prepare delicious meals for us. I did a lot of fishing and my father taught me to be a good hunter. My mother and father loved me very much and they were kind to me. But, one day when I was a young man out hunting for food, some men captured me in a trap that they had set in the woods that bordered the beach. They put chains on me and took me to the ship that brought me to this colony." All that Sabra had left of his life in Africa was a pouch containing a few seeds from one of the plants that grew around his village, which he kept hidden under his pallet. He had been wearing the pouch on a strap tied around his waist on that day in 1619 when he had been captured.

Sabra's stories about his life in Angola with his family were so vivid that they made Daniel feel like he had been in Africa with Sabra. He thought that he could feel what it must have been like to go about the day without the fear of a master or an overseer. When he heard the stories, he could imagine the beautiful flowers and trees that grew in the forest where Sabra hunted as a boy. He could imagine the taste of the fruit that grew there, and what it must have been like to eat it and have his stomach grow full.

At the end of one of his stories about his life in Africa, Sabra told Daniel, "Daniel you are a slave with a master; but remember, no one can ever own your mind. Your mind is yours and yours alone to control, no matter what anyone else does to you or says about you. You are as free in your mind as Master Rob and Mister Joe or anyone in this world. Never let anyone make you a slave in your mind.

When I was a boy, my family had an Ox. My mother had traded some fabric that she had woven along with a few of our goats to get the ox. We brought the ox home when it was just a baby, and we began to train it to wear a harness, and to get used to being tied to a tree. The ox constantly pulled and struggled with the ropes and harness to be free of them. It became very difficult to keep it from running off. Each time that it ran away, we would find it, and bring it back to our village and tie it up again. Finally we tied a rope around the little ox and we put a large stake on the other end of the rope and drove it deep into the ground. The little ox tried and tried but he could not break free of the stake. While it was tied, the ox grew to be very large and very strong. But after a while, we noticed that it no longer struggled with the ropes, and that it had stopped trying to pull free or to run away. By this time the ox could have easily broken the ropes, overpowered us, and run away; but it didn't realize it. The ox was now trapped and bound by its mind and it had accepted the limits of captivity and servitude. He had given up."

Sabra stopped talking and looked wistful for a moment. Then he continued his speech with, "I have lived many years, and will not be with you for much longer. When I am gone, you must continue to remember what I have told you. You must always seek freedom, and promise me that you will never give up the piece of freedom that you already possess in your mind." Daniel promised Sabra, as he resolved to keep his word although, he thought as he surveyed his surroundings, that it would be a difficult promise to keep.

But hard at work on that day in June, Daniel had little time to think of Sabra's stories. Master Rob had yelled down to Mister Joe from his seat on top of his horse, "Joe, I want you to punish any one of the slaves who is not working fast. This tobacco is just like money in the bank to me. I want the best crop this year that this colony has ever seen. I don't care what you have to do. I want all of the weeds out of this field today." Mister Joe nodded his head, with a clear understanding that he had Master Rob's permission to whip as he saw fit to meet the preposterous goal of finishing that entire field that day. "It will be done by sundown boss," Mister Joe told Master Rob. Master Rob replied, "See that it is," and trotted off on Jacque, leaving a thick cloud of dust hanging in the sticky air.

Mister Joe stood at the end of the row near Sabra, holding his whip in his hand. "Y'all better get all them weeds out or you gonna see more trouble than you know what to do with, I can promise you that," he snarled and cracked his whip to make sure that the slaves understood his meaning. Daniel tried to work fast. He knew that the next time the whip cracked, it would come down hard across someone's back.

Marcus whispered, "Daniel you missing leaves. I told you to take three or four leaves off of the bottom of every plant. Then you take the hoe and chop all of the weeds down from around the plants." Marcus a short man who looked to be in his thirties, with light tan coloring and reddish hair, was excellent at agriculture and could make anything grow. He was largely responsible for the success of the plantation's tobacco crop. He had spent years perfecting the hard-to-grow plants into the hardy variety that now thrived on the plantation. He whispered to Daniel so that no one else could hear what he said. Daniel and Marcus knew that all of the slaves would be in trouble if Mister Joe found out about the weeds and leaves that Daniel had missed.

Daniel had been working in the fields for as long as he could remember. His first job was to pick off the ugly horned worms that seemed to love to eat holes in the tobacco leaves. When Daniel was seven, he pulled the weeds from around the tobacco plants with his hands. Now, at twelve, he used a hoe to chop the weeds because he was tall and strong enough to maneuver the long handled tool. He used its thin, flat metal blade to get rid of more weeds than he could have by pulling them with his hands.

It was hard work. Sometimes, Daniel's back hurt from bending over to chop the weeds. Other times, he picked so many tobacco leaves from the plants, doing what is called "priming" and "topping", that his fingers became cramped.

Right now, Daniel was hungry and thirsty. He wondered how much longer he would have to work before Mr. Joe would let them take a break. Daniel wanted a drink of water and to eat the piece of bread that Becca had given him early that morning before she left the rickety dwelling, known as the slave quarters, to go to work in Master Rob's house.

Suddenly Daniel heard Mister Joe shout, "Hey boy, you down there at the end" A startled Daniel looked up quickly and saw that Mr. Joe had begun to walk down the long row of tobacco plants towards him. *Mr. Joe is coming to get me*, Daniel thought. *I must have slowed up in my work when I was thinking about eating.* Mister Joe was getting closer. Daniel tried hard to speed up, but he was so scared that his body felt like rubber and he could not get it to cooperate with him.

Old Sabra sat and watched. He saw that Mister Joe was headed for Daniel. Mister Joe was about ten steps away from Daniel when Sabra struck his drum hard. Daniel jumped at the sound of the drum. Sabra went on beating it hard and began loudly singing, "Tobacco boy, tobacco boy, prim that tobacco. Tobacco boy, tobacco boy, top that tobacco, get down low, chop them weeds, move along quick, or you gonna feel the stick." The words of Sabra's song may have sounded harsh to someone who didn't know Sabra. But he meant Daniel no harm. He was playing loudly and singing those words in hopes of creating a distraction that would help Daniel.

But even Sabra did not plan the kind of distraction that happened next. At the sound of his drum and song, a frightened rabbit that had been hiding under some old crates along the side of the field ran out from its retreat and across the rows of tobacco plants. Jip, who was now fully awake, let out a growl and then a howl and took off in a fast run after the rabbit. He went tearing through the field barking, bending and breaking all of the tobacco plants that were in his path. Mister Joe's whip was now lying on the ground and he yelled for Jip to come back. Jip kept chasing the rabbit. He had trampled dozens of tobacco plants by now. Mister

Joe began running and chasing the dog, who was still running, although the rabbit was no longer in sight. It had probably made it into the woods by now. A few minutes later Mister Joe had to stop running because one of his feet had gone down into a shallow hole, which had caused him to lose his balance. He fell to the ground and landed on his backside.

Master Rob, who was returning from town and happened to be near, heard all of the barking and yelling. He rode over to find out what was causing so much noise. He took one look at his ruined tobacco plants and Mister Joe lying in the field, and yelled at Mister Joe, "You are fired! You and your dog get off my plantation now before I shoot the both of you!"

"It was that good for nothing Sabra's fault. He caused all this," Mister Joe told Master Rob. Sabra stood near the two men. He was old and slow, but he somehow managed to always find a way to be close enough to hear everything when something troublesome occurred. Master Rob looked down from his horse at Sabra with an angry glare. "I'll deal with you later Sabra. Marcus, you get over there and take care of those trampled plants. Everyone else, go back to where you were working before all of this mess started. I still want this field weeded today, and I'm going to sit right here and watch to make sure it gets done. Now y'all get to work. You too Sabra, no more drums. You weed today with the rest of them. If you can make trouble, you can work the fields." Master Rob snarled at Sabra. Sabra nodded his head at Master Rob, and had turned to walk back to the field with the others when he heard Mr. Joe yell at him. "Sabra, you think you got off, but I'll get you for this. You can be sure of that" Sabra looked down at the ground and continued his slow walk. He did not answer Mister Joe. Sabra knew that he had helped Daniel avoid a beating by using his drum and he was glad about that. He chuckled under his breath as he remembered the comical sight of Mister Joe lying on the ground on his back, and at the shenanigans of Jip and the frightened rabbit.

Sabra, Daniel and the other slaves resumed their grueling work. Marcus went to work on the plants that the dog had trampled. Some of the plants needed to be dug up and planted again. Others needed to be propped up with sticks. Marcus got every one of the plants taken care of while Master Rob watched his every move.

When it finally grew too dark for them to see the weeds, Master Rob told the tired slaves that they could stop working. He said, "You can knock off work now and be back at first light. Sabra, you walk over to the house and tell the Mistress that I won't be home for supper." Master Rob could have ridden Jacque to his house and delivered the message himself, but he was still angry about the damaged tobacco plants. He sent Sabra on the long walk to the house to punish him.

Daniel knew that the work that Master Rob had made them all do had been too hard for Sabra. He could tell that Sabra was very tired when they finished; and now Sabra had to walk about a mile in the dark to take a message. Although it was forbidden for slaves to look their masters in the eyes or speak to them, Daniel took a risk to help Sabra and with his head bowed, he spoke to Master Rob. Daniel said, "Begging your pardon Master, I will take the message to the mistress, if you please sir". "Boy, hold your tongue and know your place. You know better than to speak without my permission. One more word out of you and you will get this whip for sure," Master Rob angrily replied to Daniel. He turned toward Sabra and said, "Sabra, be on your way".

Later that night, Daniel was completely worn out from the long day of work in the field, he could not fall asleep. He lay in the semi-darkness on top of his pallet made of straw and rags on the dirt floor in the slave quarters; which housed all of the slaves. He inhaled the stale air in the room that smelled of body sweat, soured straw, and the last cooked meal. He was watching the patterns cast by the moonlight as it found its way into the slave quarters through the spaces between the roughhewn boards that formed the sides and roof of the quarters. He was waiting for Sabra to come back from his errand to the master's house. Daniel heard the door creak; saw it open, and watched as Sabra slowly entered. He thought that Sabra moved slower tonight than he had ever seen him move. Sabra carefully picked his path, over the sleeping slaves, to the far side of the room to his pallet and lay down. Daniel got up quietly and made his way over, careful not to awaken the others. He whispered to Sabra, "Are you alright?"

Sabra answered, "Daniel, my young friend, I am fine, just very tired. Why are you still awake? It is very late". "I could not sleep" Daniel told Sabra. "I was worried about you". Daniel leaned closer to Sabra and noticed a big bloody cut on Sabra's face. "Sabra, what happened to your face?" Daniel asked. Did Mr. Joe do that to you?" Sabra smiled and told Daniel, "That Mister Joe, he needs a whole lot of leave alone." He smiled a second time and told Daniel that the cut was not anything that he should worry himself about. "Try to get some sleep. We will have to begin work again in just a few hours," the old man told Daniel. "But, I can't sleep, Sabra. I am tired of this life. I lie awake and I think of what a dreadful life we are forced to live, no good to ever look towards." "Daniel, as I have told you many times, you are free in your mind and in your dreams. You must draw strength from the knowledge of that freedom. You must let it motivate you to survive, and consider possibilities that are beyond what you see every day, rather than to make you tired. If you tire and give up, you'll be just like that ox, and the horrors and the bondage that we are forced to live in will win and we must never let them win. We have to win for ourselves and for all enslaved people." Sabra sat up and reached under his pallet. He pulled out the pouch that he had brought with him from Africa and told Daniel, "Bring me a cup of warm water. I want to give you something that will help you." Daniel walked across the room to the fireplace where an old kettle was sitting on the hearth. The fire that was used to cook the evening meal of yams and a few mustard greens had gone out many hours ago, but the hearth was still warm and so was the water in the old kettle sitting on a shelf. Daniel poured some warm water into the cup and took it to Sabra.

Sabra opened his pouch and poured an odd-looking brown seed in the palm of his hand. He dropped the seed into the water and gently shook the cup, being careful not to spill the water. He looked at Daniel, softly smiled and passed the cup to him and said to Daniel "Here drink this". "What is it?" Daniel asked. "The seed that I put in the cup is a dream maker. I brought it with me from my home in Africa. Drink from the cup, my friend," he told Daniel. "This will help you to sleep and to feel better."

Daniel swallowed the warm slightly bitter drink and looked back at Sabra. "Go lie down now Daniel and rest." Sabra whispered lying back on his own pallet. He closed his eyes, and exhaled a long deep breath. Daniel whispered, "You get some rest too, Sabra." Daniel quietly made his way back across the dark room. Daniel was still thinking about the things that had happened that day. *I am glad that Mister Joe will not be back. I wonder what the next overseer will be like. I bet Mister Joe put that cut on Sabra's face.* Daniel closed his eyes and everything turned black and then misty white. He opened his eyes with a start.

The white mist had disappeared. It had been replaced with bright sunlight that was streaming down from the sky through the tops of a dense group of large trees. Daniel had a feeling that he was somewhere he had never been before. He sat up slowly, stood and looked around. The first thing that he noticed was a bright, yellow bird with a dark blue spot on top of its head and beautiful, long, deep green colored feathers in its tail. The bird was sitting on the lowest limb of the tree closest to Daniel. Vines with bright, orange flowers growing from their leaves covered the thick trunk of the tree. The bird stared curiously at Daniel. After it had watched Daniel for a few minutes more, it left the limb and landed on the tree stump right beside Daniel. "Hello Daniel," the bird chirped in a rich melodic voice. Daniel took a few steps back. A bird that could talk and that knew his name was frightening for him. "Have no fear Daniel, I am Balozi. I know that my ability to speak and the sound of my name must be very surprising. In your language my name means ambassador and it is my job here to keep you safe and to act as your escort. I assure you that no harm will come to you while you are in my care. We have waited a long time for you."

Daniel felt a little more at ease and asked Balozi, "Where am I?" "I cannot tell you that Daniel," Balozi said. "You must come with me now. The others are waiting," the bird told him. Daniel asked, "Where are we going?" "Not to worry my friend, we will be there soon," Balozi said. He flew ahead of Daniel, leading the way through the dense trees, down a rocky hill, across a creek, and down into a deep valley. "We have arrived," Balozi told him. Daniel followed Balozi into a very large, area that housed small buildings. There was a huge pot on a fire in the center of the clearing. There was a pit with a fire in it with some delicious-smelling meat roasting over it. A few women and men were near the fire tending the meat and stirring the pot. Balozi flew over to a tall woman and said to her, "Greetings Iya, our visitor is here". Iya, who was wearing a dress that was made of beautiful multi-colored cloth, looked up from the fire and said to Balozi "Hello Balozi." While looking in Daniel's direction, she continued to speak to Balozi, "Please show our guest to the Hall of Visitors". "Yes, Iya," Balozi replied to the bird. Balozi returned to Daniel and said, "Daniel my friend, come with me." He flew toward the row of buildings at the farthest end of the clearing. Daniel followed the bird and walked up the steps of the building into a large room. This room was like nothing that Daniel had ever seen. It had a floor that was made of a deep rich dark brown-colored wood that was so shiny that Daniel could see his reflection in it. The floor was covered with beautiful purple and white rugs woven with intricate patterns of strange animals with huge staring eyes sitting in trees. The walls were painted bright colors and filled with all kinds of drawings of people and scenes that were foreign to Daniel.

One of the walls had a large doorway in it. Through the doorway, Daniel could see a man sitting on a large mat with his back towards him. Daniel asked the bird, "Balozi, what is this building?" "This is the Hall of Visitors, Daniel. We bring all of our important guests here." "Balozi, I am just a slave. I am not an important visitor," Daniel told the bird. Balozi replied, "To the people here, you and the man that you see through that doorway are the most important visitors that have ever come here." Daniel asked, "Who is that man, Balozi?" "The man on the other side of the door is called Irin-Ajo Pada. He cannot hear us or see us," Balozi told Daniel. Daniel asked, "What is he doing?" "He is preparing to go on a long journey. Now, I must say goodbye to you. Do not leave this hall Daniel. The others will be here soon," Balozi told Daniel. Daniel called to the bird, "Wait, Balozi, who are the others?" Balozi did not answer him. The little bird flew out of the door, past Irin-Ajo Pada, and disappeared into the sky. Daniel wondered at all that he saw around him, the drawings, Balozi the talking bird, and Irin-Ajo Pada, who still sat on the other side of the doorway. I know that Balozi said that Irin-Ajo Pada cannot hear or see me, but if I could get him to, perhaps he could answer my questions, Daniel thought.

He had decided to walk outside to speak to Irin-Ajo Pada. He had just taken a few steps towards the sitting man when he heard the chime of a bell. He turned to see both the woman Balozi had called Iya and one of the men who had been tending the fire outside standing behind him. The woman asked, "Daniel, do you know who I am?" "Yes ma'am," Daniel replied, "You are Iya. I heard Balozi say your name." "You are correct, Daniel. I am Iya and this is Baba Ologbon," Iya said to Daniel, pointing to the man standing beside her. Baba Ologbon nodded his head and looked curiously at Daniel. "Hello sir", Daniel said, looking at Baba Ologbon. The man nodded and smiled. Daniel noticed that Baba Ologbon was holding a small brass chest with a large shiny stone made into its top.

Iya began to speak again. She said, "Daniel, you are from a faraway place. The world that you live in is a difficult one. We have brought you here to help you to survive in your world. You have been told that your mind belongs to you, and that it is your place of freedom for now." "Yes Iya, my friend Sabra said that", Daniel told her. "Your friend is right," Iya said. "And because you have remembered his words, we will now call you Uhuru Shujaa. In your language, Uhuru Shujaa means freedom warrior." Daniel smiled. He liked the sound of his new name. Baba Ologbon opened his chest, pulled out a silver medal hanging from a long purple cord, and handed it to Iya. Iya said to Daniel as she hung the metal around his neck, "The mark on this metal means freedom warrior. Wear it always." Daniel was surprised and proud. He thanked Iya for the medal repeatedly. Daniel thought that it was the most beautiful thing that he had ever seen. For a boy that, up to this time in his life, had never been given anything, this medal seemed like a miracle. It was hard for him to believe that it belonged to him, and he stood there looking down at it, gently touching it to make sure that it was real.

Baba Ologbon reached into his chest again and this time he pulled out a gold metal hanging from a green cord. He gave the metal to Iya. Iya clasped the metal in her hand and said to Daniel, "Uhuru Shujaa keep the words that I am about to say to you in your mind and in your heart. Hold on to them in difficult times. She said, " I am less than none; I am equal to all; I am priceless and limitless. Now, you say the words that I just said," Daniel, repeated, "I am less than none; I am equal to all; I am priceless and limitless." "Now say them again," she told him. Daniel repeated the words again. "Good, Uhuru Shujaa. These are the words that you were brought to our land to hear. Now, look at this metal," Iya, said to Daniel. "It is handsome," Daniel said.

Iya asked him, "Uhuru Shujaa, see this mark on the metal?" Daniel looked down at the metal in her hand and saw that it had three circles on it, one inside of the other with a line that passed through the middle of the circles. The line touched both ends of all three circles. "Yes Iya, I see the mark," Daniel said to Iya who stared down at him. "Trace the mark with your finger," she told him. Daniel touched the metal with his finger and followed the circles with it. Then he touched the line in the center of the circles and followed it from end to end. Baba Ologbon, who had been quiet until now said to Daniel "Think of the mark in the center of the circle as yourself, Uhuru Shujaa. The circles are the phrases that Iya told you to repeat. See how the circles surround the line? That is the way the truth of those words will always surround you. Like the line that touches the circles, you can also touch those words with your mind. You must remember that when you return home." After he spoke, Baba Ologbon lifted the cord of the metal from Iya's hand and placed it around Daniel's neck. Daniel closed his eyes and smiled.

He opened his eyes and expected to see Iya and Baba Ologbon. Instead, Daniel saw his old familiar home in the slave quarters. A confused and very disappointed Daniel found himself back on his pallet with the tin cup he had been drinking from before he fell asleep, resting on his chest. Daniel slowly looked around, wondering what had happened. He reached down and felt for the metals that Iya had given him. Sadly, his reach only yielded the tattered shirt he had been wearing when he had fallen asleep earlier that night. He thought, *Iya, Baba Ologbon, Balozi and everything that I saw and heard must have been a dream. It had all seemed so real.*

While he laid thinking about the dream and the words that Iya and Baba Ologbon had spoken to him and told him to always remember, he heard hushed cries coming from the other side of the room. It was hard to see because it was early and still dark. As he squinted and looked around again, he noticed that everyone else appeared to be up and standing over near Sabra's pallet. Daniel stood up and hurriedly moved toward the group to see what was happening.

He saw that his mother was standing closest to Sabra's pallet. She was looking down at Sabra. As he drew closer, he could make out that she had tears running down her cheeks. Sabra was lying on the pallet, silent and without motion. Daniel asked, "Mama, what is wrong?" "Daniel, do not come any closer. Sabra is no longer with us. He must have passed away from us in his sleep last night." "No," Daniel gasped. "Sabra was very old, Daniel. We all knew that he would leave us soon. We will all miss him, but we must let him rest now." Becca knew of Daniel's deep affection for Sabra. She wanted to spare him as much grief as she could. The cut Daniel had seen on Sabra's face before he drank from the cup the night before had swollen, and produced a huge, purplish-blue knot and a dark blue bruise that badly distorted Sabra's features. Becca thought that by preventing the boy from looking on the now dead body of his friend, it would help him to remember his friend, as he had known him in life. She told Daniel to go outside and wait while they prepared Sabra's body for burial.

Daniel went outside as his mother had told him to do. He sat under a big tree and thought about Sabra. Sabra had been such a good friend. *I am going to miss him,* Daniel thought. Daniel also wondered about the drink that Sabra had given him. Had it caused his dream?

As he sat there thinking, the door to the slave quarters swung open. Daniel watched several men carrying a board with Sabra's body on it slowly walk through the door. Sabra was covered in a piece of sackcloth. Becca and a few other women followed the men. They all walked slowly towards the patch of land that was the burial ground for slaves. Daniel followed the somber party and noticed that Master Rob was already at the burial place when the group arrived. He was sitting on his horse like always. Daniel also noticed that a grave had been dug. Someone must have gone ahead of the group and dug the grave. The men-carrying Sabra placed him gently down into the grave. Master Rob told them, "Finish up here and get to work." The men filled the grave with the soil that was piled beside it. They each stood there a minute to show their respect for Sabra. A few of them wept. One woman stooped and placed a bouquet of wild flowers that she had picked on the way to the gravesite on top of the grave. After a few minutes went by, the others headed off to the fields. Daniel lingered at the grave, Sabra had meant so much to him, he stood there already feeling the void that Sabra's death had created and at the same time wanting to honor his friend in some way. He thought a moment and then his dream came to mind. He bent down and drew the three-circle symbol that had been on the metal in his dream. He used a stick to etch the design in the soft dirt of Sabra's grave. After he had finished drawing the symbol he gently spoke the words that Iya had told him to remember. He said, "Sabra you were less than none; you were equal to all; you were priceless and limitless. I will never forget you." Daniel knew that Sabra could not hear him but these were the best words that Daniel knew and were all that he could offer his friend. He stood there alone for a moment longer, and slowly headed to work with the words that Iya had told him and that he had just spoken over Sabra vibrating in his mind and lifting his spirits a bit.

Just like the day before, Daniel was working in a field next to Marcus. Mr. McRoy, the new overseer, was watching him closely. Master Rob had told Mr. McRoy earlier that he wanted Daniel to learn how to grow tobacco. He planned to clear more land and increase his crop. He wanted to make sure that he would have an ample number of experts on hand to care for the finicky plants.

Daniel tried to concentrate on the things that Marcus showed him, but it was hard to pay attention. So many things had happened. He was thinking again of the strange dream that he had the night before. He remembered Balozi, Iya, Baba Ologbon and the beautiful Hall of Visitors. He also thought of the words that Iya had told him. He smiled at the thought of his name, Uhuru Shujaa. The thing Daniel remembered most about the dream was the feel of freedom that he had experienced when he had visited that strange place in his dream. Freedom was so real in the dream that it seemed like he could touch it. Before his dream, Daniel thought that he knew what freedom would feel like. To Daniel, the freedom in the dream felt different from anything that he had ever imagined. Before his dream, he thought that freedom was running, playing, and spending time the way that you please. What he learned about freedom from his dream was that it is all of that along with the feeling of belonging and of having value. In his dream, Daniel felt like he was a person who mattered. In his life on the plantation, he often felt like he was invisible. When he thought about Sabra's death, he felt like the people that owned him never really saw Sabra or him. To them, they were slaves whose only value was the work that they performed for them; nothing more than something that had been purchased or born there for their convenience to be used until there was no more life left in them. If their owner saw them in any other way, it seemed on most occasions to be with contempt and mistrust simply because they looked different from them. They never at any time saw them as persons that were their equal. A person with hopes, dreams, and feelings. In his dream, Daniel had been able to walk with his head held high. He could look anyone in the eye and tell them what he was thinking. He did not have to wait for someone to give him permission to talk. He was equal to all and valued for who he was. To Daniel, that became the true meaning of freedom.

Daniel was still thinking of the dream when the faint *tat, tat, tat* of what sounded like a drum caused him to glance around the field. When he heard the sound, he thought of Sabra, but reminded himself that Sabra was not there. He went back to his work and again he thought that he heard the familiar *tat, tat, tat, rat, tat* of Sabra's drum. He glanced around. "Get back to work, Daniel," Marcus whispered. "I heard that this new overseer is a strict man, and he'll be watching us." "Don't you hear something that sounds like Sabra's drum, Marcus?" Daniel asked. "Drum, no I don't hear no drum. Sabra is gone. I know it's hard on you, but he is gone. Now, you best forget about him and get back to work before there is trouble."

Daniel obediently went back to his work and quietly finished weeding the long row of tobacco plants. He took a long breath, and raised one hand to his brow to wipe away the sweat that had collected there. With the other hand, he lifted the hoe and began to strike the ground. He stopped suddenly because he heard that *tat, tat, tat, rat, tat* sound again. This time, the sound was louder and it seemed to be coming from above. Daniel looked up toward the sky and dropped his hoe. There up in the clouds, when the mist cleared he could see Irin-Ajo Pada, the man from his dream, sitting with his back to Daniel, just as he had done in the dream. Iya the lady that had given him his new name and Balozi, the bird, were there with him. Daniel could not believe what he saw and stood staring up at the threesome. Irin-Ajo Pada stood up and slowly turned to face him, and Daniel realized that this mysterious man from his dream was his old friend Sabra. He stood smiling down at Daniel. He was dressed in a beautiful cape, like the one the man in the portrait in Master Rob's parlor had been wearing. Sabra wore a gold crown on his head and gone was the bloody cut that had disfigured his face the last time Daniel had spoken to his friend. Daniel did not know what to think. He looked around to see if anyone else appeared to see the group and was even more startled when Marcus and everyone else appeared to be oblivious to what he was witnessing. They continued their work without giving the visitors any notice.

Daniel looked back up at the visitors again in time to see Balozi descending from the clouds toward him. Daniel stood mesmerized as he watched the tiny bird draw closer to him. Balozi landed on Daniels' shoulder and chirped, "Greetings, Uhuru Shujaa." "Hello Balozi," Daniel said to the bird.

"After I awoke from my dream, I never thought that we would meet again. I thought that Sabra was dead, and I never expected to see Iya and Irin-Ajo Pada again either," Daniel told him. "And now you are here with me, and Sabra is not dead, he is Irin-Ajo Pada. How did you all get here?"

Balozi turned to explain to Daniel, "Well Daniel, I know that all these things may seem strange to you, but sometimes when you sleep and dream, that dream can become more than a dream." The bird went on, "When Irin-Ajo Pada or Sabra as you call him was sitting in the Hall of Visitors in preparation for his journey, he was uneasy and not able to achieve the peace that is necessary to make the journey. When Iya asked him what prevented him from his peace, he told her that he was troubled about your future. He was filled with regret for you. He told her that he could not rest peacefully unless you were free too. That is why you were brought to the Hall of Visitors. Iya thought that by giving you the new name, the metals, and the words to help you survive, she would be giving you a better life and Irin-Ajo Pada his peace. When you left the Hall of Visitors and woke up from your dream, the power of your dream for freedom and Irin-Ajo Pada's wish for your freedom were so strong that they brought us here to you. Now, you will forever have the freedom that you and Irin-Ajo Pada seek."

Daniel did not understand what Balozi had meant, but he knew how badly he wanted his freedom. He wanted it more than anything. He peered up into the sky and saw Sabra looking down, smiling a big, wide smile. It was the kind of smile that made Daniel feel at ease. Sabra sat back down and Iya told him to play the drum. Sabra began playing his drum, making a lively beat and to the beat he sang, "Tobacco boy, tobacco boy, dream of freedom. Tobacco boy, tobacco boy, fly away, flyaway home." As the drum beat and Sabra sang, Balozi asked Daniel if he was ready. "I am ready," Daniel told the bird. "Close your eyes and say the words that Iya told you to remember in your dream Uhuru Shujaa. When you feel your wings, take off." "My wings?" Daniel asked with a questioning look at the bird." Balozi looked patiently at him and began to speak, "Uhuru Shujaa, today freedom has come to visit, but it will come no closer than those clouds. If you want it, you must find the courage to rise up to it. Iya and Irin-Ajo Pada believe that you have the courage to go and get your freedom, but only you know if you really have it. If you are courageous enough to do it, close your eyes and say the words that Iya told you to remember." Daniel shut his eyes tightly. The small bird began flying in circles around Daniel. When he had flown around Daniel three times, he flew up into the air and landed back down on Daniel's shoulder. "Now Daniel, with your eyes still closed, lift your wings." This time, Daniel asked no questions. He concentrated and yelled, "I am less than none; I am equal to all; I am priceless and limitless." He tried to lift up and down where he imagined his wings to be and noticed that the air felt like it was swirling around him. With his eyes still closed, he could feel the air under his wings lifting him up and up. What he couldn't see until Balozi bid him to open his eyes, was the beautiful pair of iridescent wings made of large red, blue, green, and white feathers that had grown from his body, above his arms. He saw too that he had landed in the clouds with Iya and Sabra. "Welcome, Uhuru Shujaa," Sabra told him. "It is good to see you again, my young friend." Daniel greeted his friend with a handshake and Iya with a bow. He thanked her profusely for giving him his freedom and his wings. "You are most welcome, Uhuru Shujaa," Iya said to Daniel.

Daniel was elated and wasted no time learning how to use his new wings. He flapped his wings and took off. He whirled, twirled, and practiced somersaults. He learned to sail on the wind, and he soared with the majesty of an eagle. He dove down towards the ground and then back up to the heights of the clouds, landing a short distance away from his friends. With a leap, he took off again, this time he landed next to Iya, Sabra, and Balozi. For Daniel, this new kind of freedom was understandably amazing. With his new wings, Daniel had not only left behind slavery, with its horrific confinement of masters and overseers; and inequality at all levels. He had also transcended the restraints of walking, and the life of confinement to the earth. He now had a kind of freedom that no one else had ever received. He had been given true freedom, even more than what Sabra had always wished for him.

Now back with his friends again, Daniel told Iya, "You've done so much for me. You've given me my freedom and these wings. And Balozi you helped me to discover my courage. I owe you both so much. "You owe us nothing Daniel. I always knew that you had the courage that it took to be free," Balozi told him. Daniel flew up and around them testing his wings again. They all watched him fly. It looked like he floated on the wind, like a being that had always flown.

This time, when Daniel rejoined the others Iya told him, "It was your dream that searched for freedom. It was your courage that brought you to it. Now that you have it, cherish it always and try to help others with it. I must return to my world and my work at the Hall of Visitors. Others need my assistance with their journeys. Before I leave, I want to return to you some things that belong to you."

Iya reached into her pocket and retrieved the two medals that she had given to Daniel in his dream and she hung them around Daniel's neck. They made a clanging sound when they landed together on his chest. Daniel was overjoyed. He had not expected to ever see the metals again. "Come, Balozi, it is time for us to leave. Baba Ologbon waits for us," she told the bird. Daniel was very grateful for all that the bird and Iya had done for him. He wished that they would stay with him and Sabra for a while, but he understood that their work called them back to their world. He said goodbye to the pair and the two disappeared into the mist of the clouds.

Sabra remained in the clouds, but after many days of traveling and exploring, Daniel returned to the plantation for Becca. He found her when she was on her way to work early one morning. When he saw her, he told her, "Mama, I have come to take you to freedom." He told her that his new name was Uhuru Shujaa and that his name meant freedom warrior and he showed her his new wings. Becca was frightened at the sight of her winged son. When Daniel had not come home, Becca had thought that she would never see him again. She was alarmed and hoped that he had managed to escape. She dared not make mention of his absence for fear of alerting the authorities who would look for him and force him to return to the plantation. But what she didn't know was the master had hired a man named Henry Beckwell to do just that. Beckwell, a trained tracker was searching high and low for Daniel but could not find a trace of him anywhere. When many days passed and Daniel didn't return, Becca thought that something horrible must have happened to her son. When she first saw Daniel standing there in the early light, she believed him to be a phantom of some sort. Daniel explained to his mother that she should not fear him, "I am the same Daniel, I just have wings now," he couldn't help but smile and Becca smiled back at him. He told her about Sabra, Iya and Balozi. He told her about his dream, the words that Iya had spoken to him, about courage and about what it felt like to fly. Becca was still skeptical, but she decided to trust her son and gently touched his face with her hand. Daniel told her to hold tight to him and he lifted the two of them off of the ground and high above the trees. He landed in the yard of a man that he had learned about in his travels; a man who along with his wife helped slaves to get to places where they could live in freedom. They promised to help Becca. Now satisfied that she was in good hands, Daniel hugged Becca tightly for a moment and told her goodbye and that he would look in on her from time to time and then he returned to his new home, the sky.

Neither Daniel or Sabra ever saw Iya and Balozi again. Some people say that they can still hear Sabra playing his drum and singing, "Tobacco boy, tobacco boy, dream of freedom. Tobacco boy, tobacco boy, flyaway home." Others say that on some hot, hazy days, they have caught sight of a boy with beautiful wings soaring high above in the clouds; and that sometimes, he ventures down to earth to help those who are courageous and have powerful dreams of finding their freedom.

The End.

About the Author

Beverly Harris grew up in coastal Virginia and discovered her love of books at an early age. She spent many Saturday afternoons in the local public library reading and learning about the world through books.

After college Beverly lived and worked in Korea, Italy, and Washington, DC. She continued to enjoy reading and began to write, thinking of her writing as a tool to teach, entertain, and inspire the imaginations of others.

In her free time 'Bev' likes gardening, photography and travel. She enjoys visiting museums and of course libraries.

Afterword

1619 was the beginning of many new things in the small British colony of Virginia. But not all of these new beginnings were good ones for either the people who lived on the land before the British arrived, or for those who would come to inhabit it in the first two hundred years that followed.

In particular, a pirated ship of young Africans arrived on a hot day in August 1619—the beginning of a long-forced migration. Their labor, and the labor of the millions of black people who resided and worked in North America as unfree people, helped to build what would become the most powerful nation in the world.

These people, however, paid an enormous price for their status as bonded workers. Treated first as servants, and then as slaves with little chance of gaining freedom, these men, women and children suffered brutality, want and inequality throughout their lives. Still, they insisted on surviving, gaining freedom for themselves and their families, and becoming true citizens within the nation. Their stories are an integral part of American history that every child, and adult, should know. This wonderful book is a gentle introduction to their tragic, but at times triumphant, history as Americans.

Dr. Brenda E. Stevenson, UCLA

Author of Life in Black and White and What is Slavery

www.ingramcontent.com/pod-product-compliance
Lightning Source LLC
Chambersburg PA
CBHW060345080526
44584CB00013B/925